WHAT'S HAPPENING TO TOM?

OTHER BOOKS ABOUT TOM AND ELLIE

Tom Needs to Go
A book about how to use public toilets safely
for boys and young men with autism and related
conditions
ISBN 978 1 84905 521 5
eISBN 978 0 85700 935 7

Things Tom Likes
A book about sexuality and masturbation for boys
and young men with autism and related conditions
ISBN 978 1 84905 522 2
eISBN 978 0 85700 933 3

Ellie Needs to Go
A book about how to use public toilets safely for
girls and young women with autism and related
conditions
ISBN 978 1 84905 524 6
eISBN 978 0 85700 938 8

Things Ellie Likes
A book about sexuality for girls and young women
with autism and related conditions
ISBN 978 1 84905 525 3
eISBN 978 0 85700 936 4

What's Happening to Ellie?
A book about puberty for girls and young women
with autism and related conditions
ISBN 978 1 84905 526 0
eISBN 978 0 85700 937 1

BY THE SAME AUTHOR

Sexuality and Severe Autism
A Practical Guide for Parents, Caregivers and Health
Educators
ISBN 978 1 84905 327 3
eISBN 978 0 85700 666 0

WHAT'S HAPPENING TO TOM?

A book about puberty for boys and young men with autism and related conditions

KATE E. REYNOLDS

Illustrated by Jonathon Powell

Jessica Kingsley *Publishers*
London and Philadelphia

First published in 2015
by Jessica Kingsley Publishers
73 Collier Street
London N1 9BE, UK
and
400 Market Street, Suite 400
Philadelphia, PA 19106, USA

www.jkp.com

Copyright © Kate E. Reynolds 2015
Illustration copyright © Jonathan Powell 2015

Library of Congress Cataloging in Publication Data
Reynolds, Kate E.
  What's happening to Tom? : a book about puberty for boys and young men with autism and related conditions / Kate E. Reynolds ; illustrated by Jonathon Powell.
     pages cm
  ISBN 978-1-84905-523-9 (alk. paper)
  1. Teenage boys--Growth. 2. Teenage boys--Physiology. 3. Puberty. 4. Children with autism spectrum disorders--Health and hygiene. 5. Youth with autism spectrum disorders--Health and hygiene. I. Powell, Jonathon, illustrator. II. Title.
  RJ143.R49 2015
  618.92'85882008351--dc23
                              2014015129

British Library Cataloguing in Publication Data
A CIP catalogue record for this book is available from the British Library

ISBN 978 1 84905 523 9
eISBN 978 0 85700 934 0

Printed and bound in China

With many thanks for the expertise,
support and humour of surgeon
Mr Jamie McIntosh and his team at
the Royal United Hospital, Bath.

Also for my children,
Francesca and Jude.

Kate

Thanks to Sarah Attwood for
the opportunity and support
that led to these books.

Jonathon

A NOTE FOR PARENTS AND CAREGIVERS

The changes that take place during puberty can be alarming to any young person, but those with severe forms of autism rely on routines and can find any change difficult. This book shows pictorially what physical changes occur and explains that these are the same for typically developing young men and those with autism. A potential source of worry for many of our young people is that these changes will happen suddenly, even overnight. Some young men can't sleep for fear of waking up as a man. Tom's story emphasises how gradual these changes will be.

This book describes 'nocturnal emissions' or 'wet dreams' as natural events that happen in the lives of all young men during puberty (and occasionally beyond this point). The central character, Tom, shows how to deal practically with this event and not be alarmed. Finally, the book reassures boys and young men with autism that, although their penises may enlarge and become hard, this is temporary.

The overall message is that changes during puberty are natural to all boys as they gradually become young men. The final page demonstrates that maturing can bring welcome changes, such as wearing more 'grown up' clothing and shaving or using body spray (emulating an admired male in their lives).

Tom is having a shower when he sees a hair on his testicle. He pulls it, but it is attached. The hair is part of Tom.

Tom used to worry that he would wake up one day covered in hair. But now he knows that the hairs will grow slowly.

Some of these hairs, like the ones on his face, can be shaven when the time is right. The other hairs that don't get shaven will stop growing after a while. They won't grow longer and longer forever.

Tom's face looks different because he has lots of spots. They hurt his face a bit and sometimes make it red. Tom knows that the spots will slowly go away as he grows into a young man.

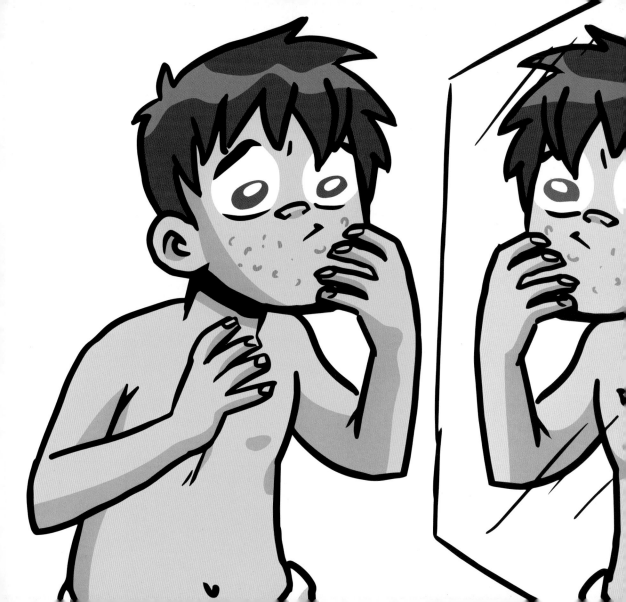

Tom's voice has been a bit strange recently, too. It's been wobbling up and down. Sometimes it sounds deep, like his father's voice. Tom doesn't know how his voice will sound when he tries to speak! But he knows that his voice will be lower all the time eventually, just like other young men.

As all these changes happen, Tom also starts to smell a bit different. Sometimes he doesn't smell nice at all! Tom knows to shower or bath every day and put on deodorant so he smells fresh. Mmmm.

Sometimes when he is sleeping, Tom's penis gets hard and leaks white liquid called sperm from the end. This makes his pyjamas and bed sheets wet.

This happens because Tom is growing into a young man and his penis is getting bigger. This is the same for all boys.

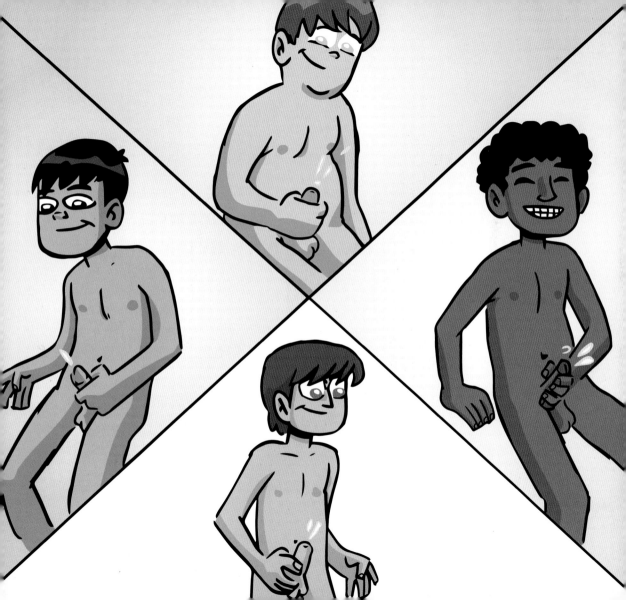

Tom knows to take off his wet pyjamas and have a shower or bath to get clean.

Tom knows to remove the bed sheets and put them in the laundry with his pyjamas.

Sometimes Tom's penis gets harder and bigger when he is excited but it will get softer and smaller again.

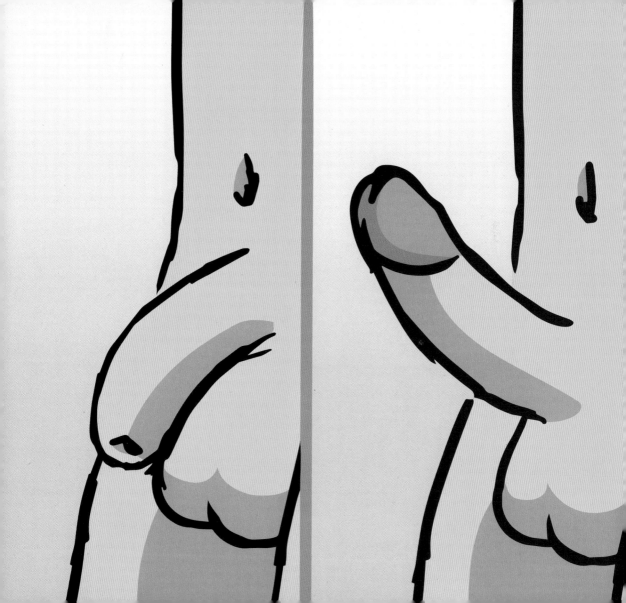

Tom remembers that all these changes will happen gradually, like a snail sliming along the length of a soccer pitch.

All these things happen because Tom is growing up into a young man. He started as a baby, grew into a little boy, then a bigger boy and now is becoming a young man.

Tom wants to grow up so he can do new things. Tom knows he will be able to wear different clothes, shave like his father does and stay up later at night when he's grown into a young man.

ABOUT THE SERIES

Sexuality and sexual safety are often difficult subjects for parents, caregivers and health educators to broach with young people who have severe forms of autism and related conditions. These young people are widely perceived as being 'vulnerable', but the lack of sex education and social opportunities available only increases that vulnerability, leaving them open to child sex and other abuse. Unlike typically developing children who learn by 'osmosis' from their peers, our young people need clear and detailed information provided by those who support them.

This is one of a series of six books – three addressing issues for boys and young men and three for girls and young women. Each book tells a story about the key characters, Tom and Ellie, giving those supporting young men and women something tangible as a basis for further questions from young people. The wording is unambiguous and avoids euphemisms that may confuse readers and listeners. Many young people with severe forms of autism and related conditions are highly visual, so the illustrations are explicit and convey the entire story.

These books are designed to be read with a young person with autism, alongside other more generic reading material.